The Time Capsule

Robert Campbell

About this Book

For the Student

Listen to the story and do some activities on your Audio CD

Talk about the story

beat• When you see the blue dot you can check the word in the glossary

K Prepare for Cambridge English: Key (KET) for Schools

For the Teacher

HELBLING e-ZONE THE EDUCATIONAL PLATFORM A state-of-the-art interactive learning environment with 1000s of free online self-correcting activities for your chosen readers.

Go to our Readers Resource site for information on using readers and downloadable Resource Sheets, photocopiable Worksheets and Answer Keys. Plus free sample tracks from the story.

helbling.com/english

For lots of great ideas on using Graded Readers consult Reading Matters, the Teacher's Guide to using Helbling Readers.

Level 2 Structures

Past simple of *be*	Comparative
Past simple	Comparative with *as...as*
Past simple (common irregular verbs)	Superlative
Be going to	*To* for purpose
Past continuous	Adverbs of manner
Past simple v. past continuous	*A lot of, not much, not many*
Past simple in questions	*And, so, but, because*
Have to / must	Possessive pronouns
Mustn't	

Structures from lower levels are also included

Contents

HELBLING DIGITAL

INTERACTIVE ONLINE TEACHING AND LEARNING MATERIALS

e-ZONE
THE EDUCATIONAL PLATFORM

HELBLING e-zone is an inspiring new state-of-the-art, easy-to-use interactive learning environment.

Use the **personal access code** on the inside back cover of this book to unlock a host of self-correcting activities, including:

- reading comprehension;
- listening comprehension;
- vocabulary;
- grammar;
- exam preparation.

TEACHERS register free of charge to set up classes and assign individual and class homework sets. Results are provided automatically once the deadline has been reached and detailed reports on performance are available at a click.

STUDENTS test their language skills in a stimulating interactive environment. All activities can be attempted as many times as necessary and full results and feedback are given as soon as the deadline has been reached. Single student access is also available.

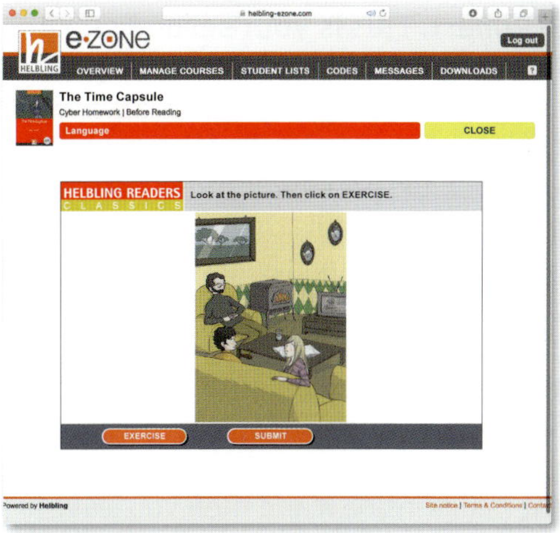

1000s of free online interactive activities now available for HELBLING READERS and your other favourite Helbling Languages publications.

ONLINE ACTIVITIES

helbling-ezone.com

helbling.com/readersblog

Love reading and readers and can't wait to get your class interested? Have a class library and reading programme but not sure how to take it a step further? The Helbling Readers BLOG is the place for you.

The **Helbling Readers BLOG** will provide you with ideas on setting up and running a Book Club and tips on reading lessons **every week**.

- Book Club
- Worksheets
- Lesson Plans

Subscribe to our **BLOG** and you will never miss out on our updates.

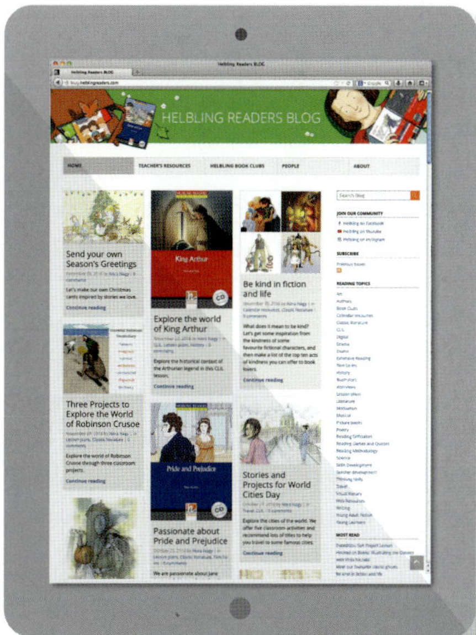

Meet the Author

Hello Robert. This is your second story for Helbling Readers Red Series.
That's right. The first story was called *Next Door*. It was about a boy called Eoin and a twin brother and sister who move into the house next door. People think they come from another planet and Eoin wants to discover the truth.

Is this story very different?
I hope so. This story is about a girl called Jan. Her history teacher gives the class a project to make a time capsule. A time capsule is a container. You put things inside it and then you leave it in a special place for people to find in the future.

What happens?
I can't tell you! Read the story to find out. I think it's fantastic when you read a book or watch a film and you don't know what happens.
I had a lot of fun writing this story because it takes place in different times and lots of things happen. I wonder how many readers can predict the ending.

What genre is it?
Both *Next Door* and *The Time Capsule* are *fantasy stories*. They have elements of *science fiction* too, but I wanted them to be about real people the reader can identify with.

Have you ever made a time capsule?
No, I haven't. But I hope one day I'll find one. I think it's fascinating discovering about people's lives in the past. I think the lives of ordinary people are often more interesting than the lives of the famous people we read about in history books.

Before Reading

1 Match the containers with the names.

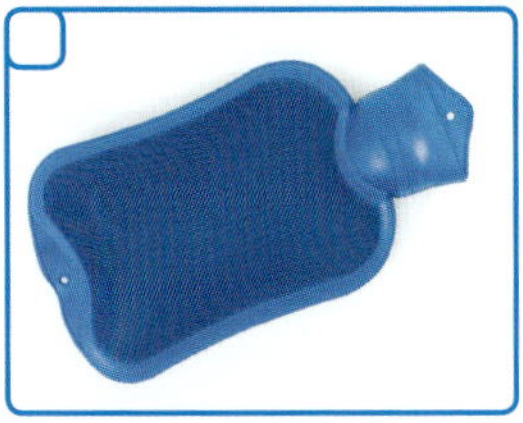

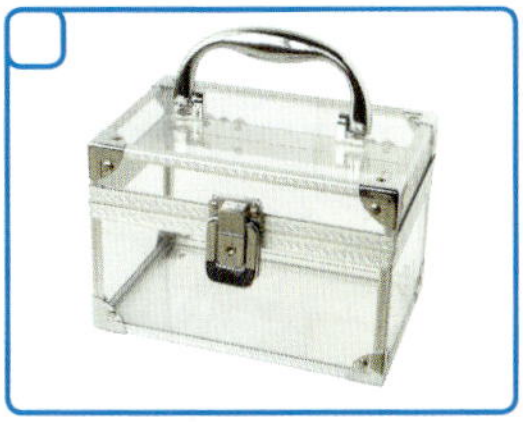

a biscuit tin
b bottle
c cup
d drawer
e glass
f glass case
g hot water bottle
h plastic bag

2 Think of something to put inside each container.

3 A *time capsule* is a container. You put things inside it and then leave it in a special place for people to find in the future. Which of the containers on this page is best for a time capsule?

Before Reading

1 **People put things inside time capsules to give information about the present time. Read this list of things. Do you associate them with the past, the present or the future?**

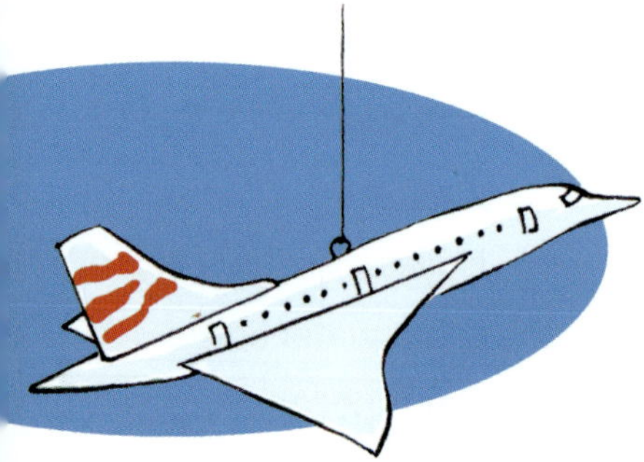

- 3D
- black and white television
- Concorde
- flying taxis
- holidays in space
- MP3 players
- *Twilight*
- robots
- vinyl LP records
- mobile phones

PAST	PRESENT	FUTURE

2 **Add one more thing to each category from exercise 1.**

3 **In the book the main character, Jan travels through time. Imagine you can travel through time. What period do you want to travel to: the past or the future? Write why you choose this time period.**

Ask a partner.

4 **Jan's favourite television programme is *Doctor Who*. Listen to the description then tick (✔) true (T) or false (F).**

		T	F
a	Doctor Who is America's favourite television series.	☐	☐
b	Doctor Who first started in 1963.	☐	☐
c	The Doctor is an alien.	☐	☐
d	The Doctor can travel through time and space.	☐	☐
e	The Doctor's time machine is called a DALEK.	☐	☐
f	His time machine looks like a police car.	☐	☐
g	His time machine is very big inside.	☐	☐
h	The Doctor looks like an alien.	☐	☐
i	The Doctor can regenerate if he is killed or injured.	☐	☐
j	The Doctor's enemies are called DALEKS.	☐	☐

Before Reading

1 Look at Jan's story.

2 Here are the first lines of Jan's story. Put the words in the right place and then check your answers on the next page.

at for inside into of to

"When Jan walks **a** .... the kitchen, her mum is sitting **b** .... the table, reading a book and drinking a cup **c** .... tea. Jan goes **d** .... the fridge and looks **e** .... **f** .... a drink."

3 What happens next? In groups of 4 continue the story. Each person writes a sentence.

4 Listen to these characters from the story. Number the pictures.

a

b

c

d

APPLE
JUIC

Thursday, 25 February 2010

AN OLD BISCUIT TIN

When Jan walks into the kitchen, her mum is sitting at the table, reading a book and drinking a cup of tea. Jan goes to the fridge and looks inside for a drink. It's a choice between a cola and an apple juice. The apple juice wins.

"Don't eat anything," mum says. "Dinner's in 20 minutes."

Jan doesn't answer. She takes a glass from the cupboard above the sink, sits down opposite mum, and pours the apple juice into the glass.

"Mum?"

"Uh-huh?"

Mum doesn't look up from her book. It's always the same. When she starts reading a book, she can't stop until she reaches the end. It makes dad mad.

"Can you give me something for my time capsule?"

Mum looks up from her book. Suddenly she's interested.

"Your *what*?"

"My time capsule. It's for a school project."

"What's a time capsule?"

Jan can't believe her mum doesn't know what a time capsule is. Everyone knows what a time capsule is.

"A time capsule… you know."

"No, I don't know."

GLOSSARY

- **a choice:** possibility to decide
- **fridge:** place to keep food cold
- **pours:** puts liquid into a glass
- **reaches:** comes to; arrives at

"You put things inside it and then you bury• it in the garden for someone to find in the future. That's why it's called a time capsule."

Mum puts down her book. She drinks some more tea and looks across• at Jan.

"What do you put inside?"

"Things. Personal things... a letter... things related to• now... this year... a diary or a newspaper, for example." Jan looks at the apple juice. "Or a bottle of apple juice. When the person finds the time capsule in the future they can discover things about the past. They can read the newspaper. They can find out• what people ate and drank, and they can find out about... me."

"How do you know someone is going to find it?"

"I don't."

"I see. And this is a school project?"

"Yes. It's for History. For Mrs Zinger."

"And you want me to give you something to put inside the time capsule?" Jan makes a face. It's a face mum recognises. It's the face Jan makes to say mum doesn't understand. Mum *never* understands.

GLOSSARY

- **across:** on the opposite side of the table
- **bury:** put under the ground
- **find out:** discover
- **related to:** connected to; that describe

"No, mum. You don't understand. I want something to put the things into. I need a container•. Have you got anything? Please?"

"What kind of thing?"

"I don't know. A box? I need something strong to protect the things inside."

Mum looks around the room and thinks. Suddenly she has an idea. She goes to one of the cupboards and takes out a large old biscuit tin•. "Here it is," she says, opening the tin and looking inside.

- **biscuit tin:** metal box for biscuits
- **container:** something to keep things inside

Jan remembers the old biscuit tin with its bright• pictures of traditional winter scenes from a perfect past.

She remembers looking at the pictures of the children playing in the snow, the family sitting around a living-room fire, the boy and girl building a snowman•, the shop windows in the village street, the man carrying a Christmas tree home.

She remembers thinking about the lives of the people in the pictures. Where did they live? What were their names? And she remembers the name written in big red letters across the top of the tin. *McInytres: Britain's Best Biscuit Company.*

MEMORY

What things do you remember from when you were a child?

GLOSSARY

- **bright:** with lots of colours; shining
- **snowman:** human figure made of snow

Now Jan's mum is making a face. She's looking inside the tin and she doesn't like what she sees. She opens the organic recycling bin• and throws away some old forgotten biscuits. Then she cleans the tin and gives it to Jan.

"You always liked this old biscuit tin. Is it OK for your time capsule?"
"Thanks, mum. It's perfect."

Mum remembers something. She goes through to the living room and comes back with a newspaper.
"It's today's newspaper. Don't tell your dad."

Jan takes the biscuit tin and newspaper up to her room and puts them on her bed. What other things can she put in the time capsule?

HELP JAN

What does Jan put in her time capsule?
Think of three things.

1 ....

2 ....

3 ....

• **organic recycling bin:** rubbish container for food. The food decomposes and can be used as fertilizer.

She looks around the room. There's her collection of *Twilight* books and DVDs. No. She wants to keep them.

How about a memory stick•? She can put all her photos on the memory stick. What a great idea! The people in the future can see all her pictures. So, Jan logs on• to her computer and copies her photo collection onto the memory stick.

What other things? There's her *Pirates of the Caribbean* collection including Jack Sparrow, Will Turner and Elizabeth Swann action figures. Yes. Why not? She's not into *Pirates* since she discovered Bella and *Twilight*. Vampires are more fun than pirates.

GLOSSARY

- **logs on:** connects to the Internet
- **memory stick:** it connects to your computer to store data

There's the postcard from aunt Suzie. She sent it to Jan's mother from Berlin in 1989. Jan's aunt was a reporter• for a newspaper in London. OK.

And the packet• of sweets she bought yesterday.

And the map of the town she printed from the Internet. People in the future are going to be interested in a map of the town from the past.

And the Kiwi key ring• dad is always telling her to use.

The Mika CD from her birthday... the Earth Hour wristband... and a copy of *TM: Teen Magazine*. Perfect. She puts them all into the box and then sits down in front of her computer.

"Now the difficult part," she says to herself. "A letter to the person in the future. What can I say?"

- **key ring:** ring to hold keys
- **packet:** small bag
- **reporter:** person who writes for a newspaper.

Thursday, 25 February 2010

JAN'S MESSAGE

Dear Sir, Madam, Miss, Ms•, friend, person from the future, alien from another planet,

My name is Jan. That's short for• Janet. My aunt Suzie calls me Janet but my mum and dad and all my friends call me Jan. I'm a girl (Duh!•). I'm thirteen years old and I live in a town called Port Prime. I don't know why it's called *Port* Prime. There's no port• here. In fact, the sea is six miles away. But you probably know that.

GLOSSARY

- **Duh!:** when you say something stupid
- **Ms:** Miss or Mrs
- **port:** a place where ships stop
- **short for:** an abbreviation

It's Thursday, February 25th 2010, and this is my time capsule. I hope you like it. Mrs Zinger, our history teacher, told us to make a time capsule for a history project. She says history doesn't only consist of• old dates, wars, politicians, kings and queens from the past. It's also about the present. Our lives today are going to be tomorrow's history.

She asked us to make a time capsule and put some interesting things inside it. Then she told us to write a letter to the person who finds the time capsule in the future (that's *you*). In the letter we have to write about the things inside the time capsule and also write about our lives. I think the things in the box say a lot about my life so I'm going to write about them and tell you about my life at the same time.

SAYING WHAT YOU WANT PEOPLE TO DO

What is missing in these sentences: *to* or *not to*?

1 The teacher told us .... use mobile phones in class.

2 Mum told me .... come home early.

• **consist of:** is made of

PORT PRIME COMPREHENSIVE

Let's start with the map. This is a map of Port Prime.
I downloaded it from the Internet. The big arrow is pointing at our house. The house is at the end of Hampton Street. It's the last house in the town. It's a new house. A lot of the houses in Port Prime are very old but the houses in this part of the town are all very new.

My house is big. There's a big living room, a big dining room, a big kitchen and a big bathroom downstairs. Then there are three en-suite bedrooms on the second floor. I think 'en-suite' is a great word. It's French. It means the bedrooms have their own bathroom. I'm sure French people never talk about en-suite bedrooms. It's one of those things English people say to be superior. Anyway, there's a third floor in our house, too. Mum and dad have their office up there. I don't go to their office often.

If you look at the map you can also see my school next to the park. My school's called Port Prime Comprehensive or PPC for short. Then there's the old part of town with the church, the town hall and the train station. There's no cinema in Port Prime. There's no youth club or social centre. If you want to do anything then you have to go to Apsworth which is eight miles away. It's easy to get bored in Port Prime. There's nothing to do.

GLOSSARY

- **arrow:** symbol indicating something (see page 23)
- **downloaded:** copied from the Internet
- **superior:** more important
- **youth club:** place with activities for young people

SWORTH AIRPOR
school
STATION
my house
ort Prime
MAP

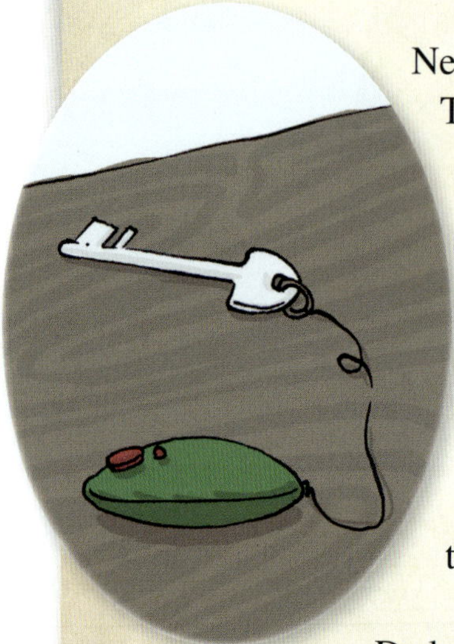

Next is the Kiwi key ring. Kiwi Technology is the name of a big company in Port Prime. Lots of people from the town work for Kiwi including my mum and dad. Kiwi makes lots of gadgets•. It makes portable music players and games consoles. Cool things. Mum and dad help to design their new products. Their work is top secret. That's one of the reasons I never go to their office.

Dad gave me the Kiwi key ring last year. It's not an ordinary key ring. Oh no. If you ever get lost•, you press the red button and it sends a signal• to another person. The other person then logs on to the Kiwi Internet site, enters• the key ring code• and can find out where you are. I got lost once. We were on holiday in Scotland. It was two years ago. Mum and dad were really scared•. So they decided to make this Kiwi key ring. It's cool, don't you think? Try it! Maybe if you press• the button I can find you in the future!

GLOSSARY

- **code:** series of numbers and letters like a password
- **enters (the code):** types
- **gadgets:** small things that use new technology
- **lost:** when you don't know where you are
- **press:** touch or push
- **scared:** frightened
- **signal:** message; sign

The newspaper is a copy of today's *Prime News*. Mrs Zinger told us to put a newspaper in the time capsule. She thinks you're interested in the news. Are you? Maybe you're more interested in the sports results. Or what's on TV tonight. I can answer that question for you. It's Thursday so it's *Doctor Who*. It's a repeat•. I saw it on Saturday but I'm going to watch it again tonight. *Doctor Who* is one of my favourite TV shows. It's about a Time Lord who travels in time. Very appropriate• for my time capsule!

DOCTOR WHO

What do you remember about *Doctor Who*? Tick (✔) the true statements.

- ☐ He comes from outer space•.
- ☐ He is a very bad alien.
- ☐ He is friendly with the Daleks.
- ☐ He uses a time machine shaped like a phone box.

I'm including my *Pirates of the Caribbean* action figures because... I love Johnny Depp. I mean I *loved* Johnny Depp. Then I discovered the *Twilight* books and films and Robert Pattinson. And anyway, I think I'm too old to have action figures now. You can have them.

- **a repeat:** a series that is on TV for the second or third time
- **appropriate:** right
- **outer space:** far in space

My Earth Hour wristband is important to me. I think we all have to do something to help the planet and stop climate change. I don't know what's going to happen to the Earth in the future but I want to do all I can to make it a good place to live. I started a recycling system at home and I help organise a Green Day at school every month. Earth Hour is a global event. People around the world turn their lights off for one hour at the same time on the same day. It sends a message to world leaders to stop climate change.

RECYCLING

Which of these things do you recycle?

- ☐ paper
- ☐ glass bottles
- ☐ mobile phones
- ☐ old clothes
- ☐ cans

What's the world like in the future? Is climate change still a problem? Are there green trees and blue skies? Are there wild animals? (I forgot to tell you – I'm a vegetarian. That's important to me too.)

GLOSSARY

- **climate change:** the change in the world's weather
- **recycling:** using something again
- **vegetarian:** person who doesn't eat meat
- **wild:** not a pet or domestic animal
- **wristband:** bracelet; something you wear on your wrist (the part of your arm above your hand)

My aunt Suzie is a news reporter. I want to be a news reporter when I'm older. She became a reporter by accident. She was in Berlin in 1989. They had a wall in Berlin that divided East and West Berlin. In 1989 the Berlin Wall came down. Aunt Suzie was there and she described the scene to newspapers. She became a famous reporter and won awards•. I'm putting her postcard in the time capsule because she is someone I respect a lot. And it's another piece of history.

The memory stick has all my photos on it. The memory stick is probably a very primitive thing in the future. How do you store• your photos? I hope you can see the photos. There are pictures of my family, Port Prime, our summer holidays and me.

Finally, some sweets in case you're hungry. And a Mika CD. It was a birthday present. I like Mika. He had a lot of problems when he was young but his music is so happy. You can read about him and Robert Pattinson in the copy of *TM: Teen Magazine* which I buy every week.

I hope you like the things in my time capsule.

Kind regards, best wishes, bye etc. etc.

Jan

- **awards:** prizes
- **store:** keep

A SCHOOL DAY

5 After dinner and after watching episode 4 of *Doctor Who* for a second time on BBC3, Jan puts her time capsule inside a plastic bag and takes it outside into the garden. She looks up at the night sky and tries to see the stars but the clouds and the light pollution• from the town make it impossible. So she watches a plane fly past on its way to Apsworth airport.

She makes a hole• in the ground beside the apple tree and puts the time capsule inside. Then she carefully covers• the hole and looks around her to check that no one is watching her. The location of the time capsule is a secret. Don't tell anyone.

Jan can see the apple tree from her bedroom window and half an hour later she's looking out of her window down at the tree and the place where she left the time capsule. She tries to imagine the scene in the future. "I wonder who's going to find my time capsule," she thinks. She looks to her left at the gardens of the other houses and then across at the fields• and the trees in front of her. "I wonder what's going to be here in the future. A shopping centre? A new university? Probably a new runway• for the airport," she thinks as another plane flies past.

GLOSSARY

- **covers:** puts something on top of the hole
- **fields:** areas of land in the country
- **hole:** empty space in the ground
- **light pollution:** when it's difficult to see the stars in the sky because of the lights of a town or city
- **runway:** the place where aeroplanes land

She goes to bed and dreams of the future. In the future Jan's house is in the middle of a big city. She looks out of her window and there are streets full of people. There are lots of tall buildings full of lights. There are shops and cinemas and a big sports stadium. She looks up and there are taxis flying in the sky. It's night but there's light and colour everywhere.

DREAMS

Why does Jan dream of the future?

Can you remember your dreams?

Tell a dream to a partner.

Friday, 26 February 2010

The next morning Jan wakes up five minutes before the alarm clock rings at seven o'clock. She remembers her dream. "The future is an exciting place," she thinks as she gets out of bed and looks out the window. The tree is still there. The other houses are still there. She isn't in the future. She's in the present and it's time to get ready for school.

She has a shower, gets dressed and goes downstairs for breakfast. Jan's dad says breakfast is the most important meal of the day but *he* never has breakfast. During the week he's always late for work or he's working on a secret project for Kiwi in his office at the top of the house. Jan can't remember the last time they all had breakfast together. Mum's in the kitchen, reading her book. She's in exactly the same position as yesterday. Jan thinks maybe mum spent the night in the kitchen, reading her book.

"Are you enjoying your book?" Jan asks.
"Not really. It's for the book group•."

Jan's mum belongs to a book group. There are five other people in the book group. They take it in turns to choose a book. When a person chooses a book, all the people in the group read the book. Then they meet at the person's house and talk about the book. Last month they all met at Jan's house. They were in the living room for hours, talking and laughing. Jan walked past the door but they weren't talking about the book. They were talking about the new family at the house down the road.

"What do you want for breakfast?" Jan's mum asks without looking up from her book. Jan doesn't answer. She always has the same thing for breakfast: a glass of fruit juice, some toast and jam, and an apple. She eats her toast and jam, drinks the juice, and takes a bite• of the apple.
"Bye, mum."
"Bye, darling. Have a good day at school."

Jan walks to school. She usually walks to the end of the road and then goes up the hill, through the centre of town to PPC. School starts at 8:45 with morning assembly•. Today is Friday, the best day of the week. Jan likes Fridays because she has all her favourite classes – English, Art, Spanish, and then History.

GLOSSARY

- **book group:** a group of people who read the same book and meet to talk about it
- **morning assembly:** the time at the start of the day when all the school students and teachers meet together
- **takes a bite:** uses her teeth to eat a piece

"So....?" Mrs. Zinger, the History teacher, looks at her students.

"How many of you completed your project and made a time capsule?"

Jan holds up her hand and looks around. No-one in the class has their hand up. Oh no! Is she the only one who made the time capsule? Mrs. Zinger smiles.

"Very good, Jan. Is Jan the only person interested in making history in this class?"

Jan's face turns red. Suddenly she feels very alone.

"No."

Jan hears a boy's voice from the back of the class. She turns and looks behind her. Michael Green is holding up his hand.

"I made one, Mrs Zinger." He smiles at Jan.

"Good, Michael."

Michael Green is the son of the owner of Kiwi Technology. He's not a very popular boy because the parents of most of Jan's classmates work for his father. Mrs. Zinger stops smiling.

"All right. The rest of you must make your time capsules this weekend. Understood?"

"Yes, Mrs. Zinger," the class says.

After class Jan sees Michael standing in the corridor. She walks up to him.

"Hi Michael. So what did you put in your time capsule?"

"Nothing."

"I don't understand."

"I didn't make a time capsule."

"But you said – ."

"I know."

"So why – ?"

"I know how it feels to be alone."

ALONE

Have you ever felt alone?

Why did you feel alone?

What did you do?

TRESPASSING

6 Jan is in her room, standing at her window, looking down at the tree, and thinking about Michael. "He's nice," she thinks. "Why doesn't he have any friends?"

She's still thinking about Michael when the sky becomes dark and the black storm clouds appear. Suddenly there's a flash of lightning• and a crash of thunder•. The electric lights in the house flicker• on and off. 'What's that?' Jan thinks she sees a shadow• moving under the tree. Yes. There's a boy standing under the tree. Jan knows that it's dangerous to stand under a tree in a thunderstorm. She knocks on the window but the boy doesn't hear her. She takes her anorak• from behind the door and runs downstairs, through the kitchen and out the back door.

"Hello?" she calls but the boy doesn't answer. She looks across at the tree but the boy isn't there. "Where are you? I know you're there!"

Jan puts up her anorak hood• and runs across to the tree. She looks around her but she can't see the boy. Did she imagine him? Then she looks down and sees the hole under the tree – the hole where she buried her time capsule. The capsule is gone•. "The boy took my time capsule." She shouts• into the darkness. "I know you're there! Come back!"

GLOSSARY

- **anorak:** jacket to protect you from the rain
- **crash of thunder:** the loud sound you hear in a storm
- **flash of lightning:** the bright light you see in the sky in a storm
- **flicker:** to go on and off very quickly
- **gone:** not there
- **hood:** part of a jacket that covers your head
- **shadow:** the dark shape you see when the light is behind someone or something
- **shouts:** speaks very loudly

There's another flash of lightning and another crash of thunder. In the flash of the lightning she sees the boy again, running from the garden. She runs after him, shouting for him to stop. The boy looks back and then disappears into the trees at the end of the garden. Jan follows the path• through the trees. She knows the path well. It goes down the hill to the river. There's an old abandoned building• by the river. She's sure the boy is going there.

GLOSSARY

- **abandoned building:** a building where no-one lives
- **path:** a narrow area for people to walk along

Jan is right. When she comes to the building, she hears excited voices from inside. She looks through the broken window and sees three boys sitting on the floor, looking at the things inside her time capsule.

"Stop! Put those things back. They're mine!"

The boys look up and laugh. Then they continue going through the capsule.

"What's this, Tom?" says the boy with glasses, holding up Jan's memory stick.

"I don't know, do I? Maybe it's a knife."

"Here's a map!"

Jan walks round to the door and enters the building.

"Put those things back!"

A boy with long fair hair looks up at her.

"Girls aren't allowed in here!"

Jan laughs.

"Don't be so sexist•. And stop playing with my things."

The boy from the tree stands up. He's about the same age as Jan and has curly black hair. He looks at Jan.

"Sexist? What's that?"

"You're a sexist if you say girls can't come inside here."

The boy with the fair hair stands up and pulls the third boy to his feet.

"This is our territory•. You're trespassing•."

Jan points at the time capsule and her things.

- **sexist:** thinking men and women should be treated differently
- **territory:** an area of land that belongs to someone
- **trespassing:** going on someone else's land

"And that's my time capsule. You're stealing•."

The fair-haired boy laughs.

"Time capsule? It's a biscuit tin."

"A biscuit tin with no biscuits inside," says the boy with glasses. "Tom, I'm hungry."

Jan looks at the boy with curly hair.

"Tom? Is that your name? Please give me my things, Tom. This isn't funny. If you want, I can give you some biscuits in exchange•."

"A swap•?" asks Tom. "And where are the biscuits?"

"In my house. The house by the apple tree. The tree where you found my time... I mean, my biscuit tin."

Tom smiles. He puts Jan's things back inside the tin.

"Take us to your house. If you give us some biscuits, you can have the biscuit tin. Is it a deal•?"

Jan nods•. "OK. It's a deal."

Outside it isn't raining and there aren't any storm clouds in the sky. Jan starts climbing back up the hill. She hears the boys laughing behind her.

"She's mad, Tom."

IS JAN MAD?

Why do the boys think that Jan is mad?
Do you think that she is mad?

GLOSSARY

- **deal:** an official agreement
- **in exchange:** giving one thing for another thing
- **nods:** moves her head up and down to say 'yes'
- **stealing:** taking something from someone without permission
- **a swap:** the act of giving one thing for another thing

At the top of the hill Jan stops suddenly and looks back at them, angry.

"Why am I mad?"

Tom walks up to her.

"Because there isn't any house by the tree. There aren't any houses near here. The nearest house is Pauly's and that's half a mile down the road. Over there." Tom points back the way they just came. Now Jan laughs.

"I think *you're* mad because my house is just over..." Jan points through the trees to her house but there isn't any house. "... there!"

She doesn't understand. She looks around her to be sure she's in the right place. It looks right but everything is wrong. Her house's beautiful garden is a wild piece of land. And the place where her house stood is empty. She runs to the apple tree.

"This is the tree!"

"*My* tree," Tom says as he shows her his name carved• in the tree trunk•.

"I don't understand. You're playing a game with me. This isn't funny, Tom. Where's my home? Where's my mum and dad?"

"I don't know."

The boy with the glasses looks at his watch.

"Tom! It's after nine o'clock. My dad's going to kill me!"

The boy with the fair hair starts running back down the path.

"Come on, Pauly! Let's go. See you tomorrow, Tom!"

The two boys disappear•, leaving Jan and Tom by the tree. Tom looks around him, feeling uncomfortable•.

"I have to go too", he says. Then he sees Jan crying.

"I don't know what to do!" she says. "What's happening to me? Where's my home?!"

Tom says: "I'm sorry". He starts walking towards the trees.

"Don't go, Tom."

But it's too late. Jan is alone under the tree where she buried her time capsule.

GLOSSARY

- **carved:** written or drawn using a knife
- **disappear:** go away so that you cannot see them
- **tree trunk:** the main part of the tree
- **uncomfortable:** not relaxed

AT TOM'S HOUSE

"Do you really have no place to go?"

Jan looks up. She's sitting on the ground• under the tree and Tom is standing in front of her, holding the time capsule. Jan shakes her head.

"Then come with me. You can stay at my house tonight."

Jan gets up and follows Tom silently. They walk back through the trees, down to the river and along the road towards the old part of Port Prime. Jan looks up at the night sky. The sky is beautiful. It's clear• and there are thousands of stars shining above her.

"How strange", she says. "Where are the aeroplanes?"

"Aeroplanes?" Tom looks surprised.

"Yes. The planes landing and taking off at the airport."

"What airport?"

"Apsworth, of course."

Jan can see that Tom doesn't know what she's talking about. She's not sure *she* understands what she's talking about. She knows she's in Port Prime but everything looks different. Maybe she's in a parallel universe•. Or maybe she's in the future. "That's it!" she thinks. "This is the future."

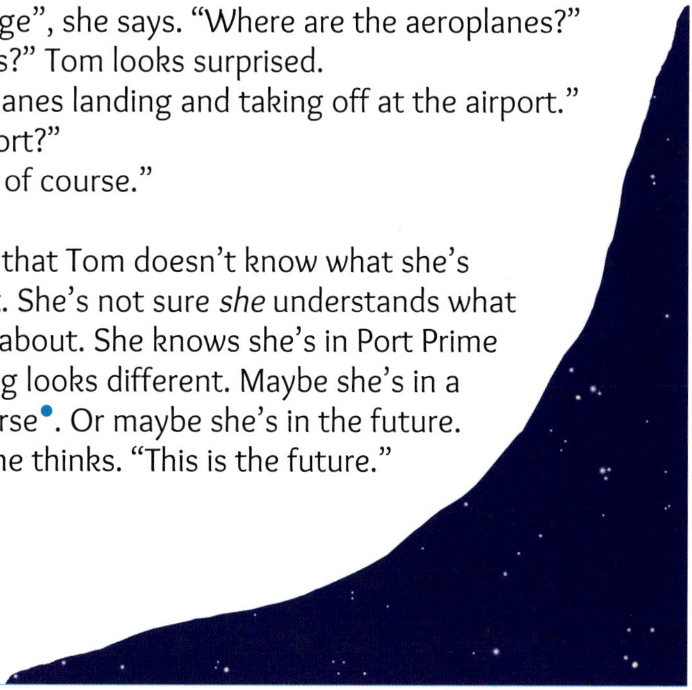

- **clear:** no clouds or pollution
- **ground:** the top part of the earth we walk on
- **parallel universe:** another world happening at the same time

She tries to remember what happened before she arrived. There was a storm. She went into the garden and stood under the tree. There was a flash of lightning. Maybe the lightning hit the tree and transported her into the future together with her time capsule. Wow!

She looks around her and thinks: "If this is the future, it's very different from the future in my dream." There aren't any tall buildings. There aren't thousands of people and lots of different colours. And there aren't any taxis flying in the sky. Maybe there was a war•. The war destroyed the airport and her home. She looks at Tom.

"Don't laugh at me, Tom. Do you promise?"
"I promise."
"I think I'm in the future."
Tom laughs.
"You promised!"
"I'm sorry. So you think you're in the future."
"Yes. But everything's different. Was there a war?"
"Yes, there was a war... but it was a long time ago."
"I think my house disappeared in the war."
"Come on, I think you need some sleep."

GLOSSARY

- **war:** two countries or parts of the same country fight

Five minutes later they arrive outside Tom's house. It's a detached house with a very old car parked outside the house and there's smoke coming out of a chimney. Tom stops and looks at Jan.

"What are we going to tell my mum and dad? We can't say you're from the past."

"No, you're right."

"No problem. I'm good at inventing stories. Listen and do what I say. OK?"

They walk up to the house and Tom opens the front door. Jan notices that the front door isn't locked. As they walk into the front hall a voice calls out from the front room.

"Tom? Is that you?"

"Yes, dad," Tom replies.

Tom walks into the front room and Jan follows. His mum and dad are sitting in two armchairs, watching television. Tom's parents look round and see Jan standing at the door.

"This is ..." Tom suddenly realises he doesn't know Jan's name. Jan helps him by introducing herself.

- **chimney:** smoke comes out of this on top of a house
- **detached house:** a house that is not attached to other houses
- **from the past:** at this moment in the story, Jan thinks she has travelled from the past into the future
- **front door:** main door of a house

"Jan. My name's Jan."

Tom's dad stands up and comes to shake her hand.

"Very pleased to meet you, Jan. Is Jan a Swedish name?"

"It's short for Janet."

"Ah. Of course."

Tom's dad looks at Tom, waiting for an explanation. Tom thinks fast.

"Jan's a friend of Pauly's. She lives in Apsworth but she missed the last bus. Can she stay here tonight? She can sleep in my bed and I can sleep on the sofa."

Tom's dad looks puzzled.

"Why can't she stay with Pauly?"

"Um.... Pauly's got a cold. He isn't well."

Tom's mum gets up and smiles at Jan.

"Well, you're welcome to stay in our house, Jan." She walks out the door saying: "I'm going to put some clean sheets on the bed."

Tom's dad invites Jan to sit down. She sits next to Tom on the sofa and looks around her at the real fire, the strange television, the patterns on the wallpaper, the pictures on the wall.

IS THIS THE FUTURE?

What do you think? Discuss with a partner.

GLOSSARY

- **missed:** was too late to take a bus or train
- **patterns:** designs with regular shapes
- **puzzled:** when somebody doesn't understand
- **sheets:** the material we sleep between in bed
- **wallpaper:** paper for covering the walls

Tom's dad tries to make conversation.
"So... where do you live in Apsworth, Jan?"
Tom answers the question.
"Near the bus station. In Lambeth Walk."
"Nice... nice. And what does your father do?"
Jan answers without thinking.
"Mum and dad both work in the research and development department of Kiwi Technology, developing new products."
Jan sees Tom looking at her, shaking his head.
"Is that right? Kiwi, you say?" Tom's dad says.
"Yes. It's the same name as the fruit."
"There's a fruit called kiwi? I didn't know. Did you know there's a fruit called kiwi, Tom?"
"No, dad."
Tom's dad looks at the biscuit tin in Tom's hands.
"What's that?"
"Nothing, dad. It's a biscuit tin."
Tom's dad looks from Tom to Jan and then back to Tom again. He knows something isn't right.
"Well... I think it's time to go to bed."

Fifteen minutes later Jan is lying in bed in Tom's room, looking out of the window at the night sky. She's frightened and excited and very, very tired. She wants to find answers to all the questions inside her head but she can't. Not now. All she can do now is close her eyes and sleep... sleep... sleep.

WHAT YEAR IS IT?

8 "This is very strange," Jan thinks. "Waking up in another person's room." Jan doesn't have any brothers or sisters. She looks around her. There are skateboard posters on the wall, a model of the Concorde• aeroplane and some books about electronics• on a shelf and a wardrobe with clothes inside. She gets out of bed and looks for Tom's computer. If she can log on to the Internet then maybe she can discover what is happening. But she can't find a computer.

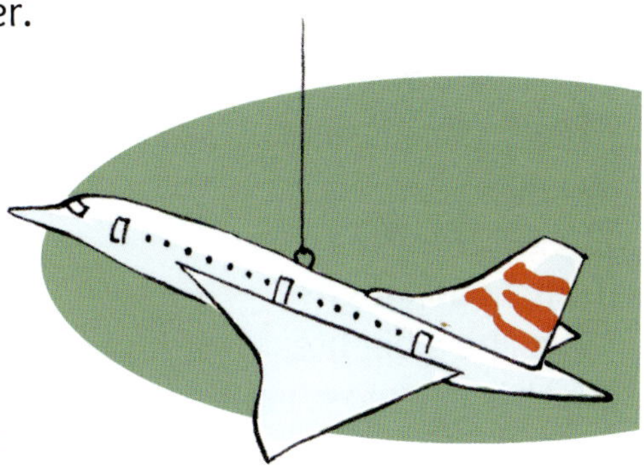

Then she remembers something. Her phone. It's in her anorak pocket. Maybe she can phone her mum and dad. She takes the phone from her anorak but there's no signal•. What can she do? Jan decides to have a shower. She goes to the bathroom but there's no shower. There's only a big bath.

She hears voices downstairs so she goes down to the kitchen. Tom, his mum and dad, are sitting at the kitchen table, eating a big breakfast.

GLOSSARY

- **Concorde:** a type of plane that flew faster than the speed of sound (see illustration)
- **electronics:** science and technology using electronic equipment
- **signal:** information sent to and received by a phone

“Morning, Jan,” says Tom’s dad. “We’re having a fry. What would you like? Sausages, bacon, eggs, fried bread...”

Jan smiles politely. She sits down at the table.

“No, thanks. I’m vegetarian.”

“What’s that?” asks Tom’s mum.

Tom answers. “Vegetarian, mum. She doesn’t eat meat.”

“That’s strange. I don’t know any vege...”

“Vegetarians.”

Tom’s dad laughs.

“We like a big breakfast, don’t we, Tom? It’s the most important meal of the day.”

Jan smiles. “That’s what my dad says. Do you have any fruit juice or cereal bars•?” They all look at her blankly•. Jan smiles. “That’s OK. Tea and toast is fine.”

BREAKFAST

Write down what you usually have for breakfast. Would you like to try a fried breakfast?

GLOSSARY

- **blankly:** without understanding
- **cereal bars:** cereal food in the shape of a rectangle

She looks across at Tom.

"Tom? Do you have a PC• or a Mac•? I can't see one in your room. If I can connect to the Internet I can..." She looks at the blank faces staring at her.

"Inter-*what*?" Tom asks.

"Inter*net*." Jan looks at the food on the table and then at the room they're sitting in. She suddenly feels very hot. Tom's mum looks worried•.

"Are you all right, love? You look ill."

Jan stands up and turns to Tom.

"Tom? Can you come with me? Please?"

She walks through to the living room and Tom follows.

"What is it?" he asks.

"What's the date?" she asks.

"February the 27th, I think."

"I mean the year. What year is it?"

"1976, of course."

"Oh, no!" Jan sits down on the sofa. "I'm not in the *future*. I'm in the *past*."

Tom sits down beside her.

"That's impossible."

Jan starts crying. She doesn't know what to do. She runs up to the bedroom, closes the door behind her, sits on the bed, and starts crying.

- **Mac:** name of an Apple computer
- **PC:** personal computer
- **worried:** anxious

When she goes downstairs, Tom's mum and dad are out shopping. Tom is sitting on the sofa, the time capsule is open next to him. He's reading Jan's letter. Then he looks up at her.

"So it's true. You're from the future."

"Do you really believe me, Tom?"

"I think so. There's just one thing I can't believe."

"What's that?"

"*Doctor Who*. Does that TV show really still exist in the future?" They both laugh.

Tom takes the memory stick from the time capsule.

"Show me your photos."

"I can't. I need a computer or a USB connection on the TV."

Then she has an idea. "Wait. I've got some photos on my phone." She gets out her phone and finds her photos.

"Is that really a telephone?"

"Yes."

"How do you dial• a number?"

"Like this. Look."

Jan sits down beside Tom and shows him her address book and the touch screen keypad•. Tom can't believe his eyes.

"And it's a camera, radio, music player, data storage device•, GPS•... I can even update• my Facebook page."

"Facebook?"

GLOSSARY

- **data storage device:** something you can use to keep digital information
- **dial:** enter the number in a phone
- **GPS (Global Positioning System):** a system for discovering exactly where you are using signals from a satellite
- **touch screen keypad:** you can touch numbers and letters that appear on the phone's screen
- **update:** add the most recent information
- **view:** the things you can see

"Forget it.... Look! Here are my photos. That's me. That's my mum and dad. That's the view• from my bedroom window. See? There's the apple tree – *your* tree. And that's PPC – the school I go to."

"It's my school too."

Tom studies Jan's phone.

"There's no cable•."

"It has a battery• to give it power. It uses aerials• for communication. Smile!"

There's a flash as Jan takes a photo of Tom. She shows him the photo.

"That's amazing. It's instant. It's like a Polaroid• camera."

"It's digital. In 2010 everything is digital."

Tom's expression changes. He speaks slowly and quietly.

"Listen, Jan. You can't tell people you're from the future. Do you understand? Not even mum and dad."

"What about your friends?"

"Especially not my friends. If you tell Jamie and Pauly then everyone in Port Prime is going to know. It's dangerous. Do you understand?"

Jan doesn't answer. She's thinking about her mum and dad. She knows they're looking for her but they're never going to find her. How can they find her if she's in the past?

"I want to go home, Tom."

JAN

Imagine you are Jan. How do you feel?

Tell a partner.

GLOSSARY

- **aerials:** a piece of equipment that receives TV or radio signals
- **battery:** an object that supplies power to a phone or other device
- **cable:** electrical wire
- **Polaroid:** a type of camera that took and printed photographs automatically

Saturday, 28 February 1976

TECHNOLOGY IS FUN

"Can you ride a bike•?"

It's Saturday morning so there's no school in 2010 or in 1976. Jan follows Tom round to the back of the house where he produces an old bicycle.

"Of course I can ride a bike," she replies confidently.

Jan can't remember the last time she rode a bicycle but they say you never forget so she gets on the bike and cycles nervously to the front of the house. Tom follows on his new red bike.

"Where are we going?" asks Jan.

"Let's go to the cliffs•. Come on!"

Tom cycles down the road and Jan follows. At home, her parents don't allow• Jan to cycle on the roads. It's too dangerous. On a normal Saturday, there are lots of cars on this road but today the road is empty. Jan feels free as she cycles faster and faster, following Tom further and further away from the town. She can see Tom pointing to the top of a hill and five minutes later they're both standing on top of the cliffs.

"Wow!" Jan looks down at the fields below. It looks so green and beautiful.

"In the future there's an airport here," she says. "Apsworth Airport."

"Really? I love aeroplanes. One day I'm going to fly to New York in Concorde. It travels faster than the speed of sound."

- **allow:** say someone can do something
- **bike:** bicycle
- **cliffs:** sides of a high land (see page 54)

"I've got some bad news. Concorde doesn't fly in 2010."

"Why not?"

"There was a bad crash•. In Paris, in 2000, I think. It stopped flying in 2003 or 2004."

"So people don't fly in the future."

"No way•. In the future everyone flies everywhere."

"But you said... "

"Concorde was fast but it was expensive. In the future flying is cheap•. There are lots of cheap airlines. People spend one weekend in Barcelona and then spend the next weekend in Athens or New York."

"Show me where the airport is."

GLOSSARY

- **cheap:** opposite of expensive
- **crash:** what happens when a car or other moving vehicle hits something
- **no way:** informal way of saying no

Jan draws the airport in the air, showing Tom where the main terminal and runways are located on the green fields. She draws the motorway that links Apsworth with the airport.

Tom listens and then says: "It's hard to imagine that this was all the sea in the past."

"The sea? Here?"

"Yes. Why do you think the town is called Port Prime? A long time ago the sea came up to these cliffs where we're standing. Then there was a big storm and the sea went away."

Jan and Tom sit down on the edge• of the cliff.

"I think this is a magic place," Tom says. "Maybe that's why you're here."

They sit on the cliffs for an hour, talking about life in the 1970s and life in the 2010s. Jan discovers that Tom's dad has a shop in Port Prime and that Tom wants to work in electronics in the future. She discovers that Jamie has problems at home. And she discovers that Pauly wants to be a pop star but has problems at school.

JOBS

What are you good at?

What do you want to be when you grow up?

• **edge:** the part at the end

Tom listens to Jan's description of Port Prime in the future and all the gadgets people have. Jan says: "It must be difficult to live without mobile phones and the Internet".

"Why? We live OK without them."

"How do you find information for school or communicate with friends?"

"There are books... encyclopaedias... and I can talk to my friends. How many friends do you have?"

"Oh, on Facebook I have 320 friends."

Tom laughs.

"How can you have 320 friends? When do you see them all?"

"I don't *see* them. They're on the Internet."

"They don't sound like real friends to me. How many real friends do you have? I mean friends like Pauly and Jamie."

"I don't know. There's... Michael."

"That's one. I don't know, Jan. Life in the future doesn't sound great. You don't spend a lot of time with your parents. You've only got one real friend. You can't go out on your own. And you can't cycle anywhere."

They both lie back on the grass, laughing.

FRIENDS

How many friends have you got?
Have you got any online friends?
What do you do with your friends?
What do you talk about?

Jan and Tom get back to the house in time for tea and sandwiches. Then they watch an episode of *Doctor Who* on television. The episode, called *The Seeds of Doom*•, stars Tom Baker as the Doctor. He has to destroy the giant Krynoid before it infects• the whole world. Jan laughs at Tom's old black-and-white television. When she asks him for the remote control•, Tom doesn't know what she's talking about. She explains that it's a gadget to change channels on the TV so you don't have to get up and change channels on the TV set. Tom doesn't understand.

"What's the point? There are only three channels."

"Three channels? Don't you have cable or satellite• yet?"

"How many channels do you have?"

"Hundreds."

"Why? What for?"

Tom's dad comes into the room and sits down on an armchair. He lights a cigarette and starts smoking. Jan wants to tell him about the dangers of smoking and the effects of passive smoking• on the other people in the room but she doesn't. Tom's right. It's best not to talk about the future with other people. It's their secret.

Tom's dad suddenly remembers something.

"I forgot to tell you, Tom," he says. "Jamie was here earlier when you were out. He came for that biscuit tin. He said you borrowed• it and he needed it back."

Jan and Tom look at each other. Jamie has the time capsule!

GLOSSARY

- **borrowed:** took and promised to return it later
- **cable or satellite:** two ways to receive TV
- **infects:** passes on an illness
- **passive smoking:** breathing smoke from other people's cigarettes
- **remote control:** device to change TV channels
- **The Seeds of Doom:** the beginning of something very bad

Saturday, 28 February 1976

MUSIC

9 Jamie's not at home so Jan and Tom go to Pauly's house. They ring the doorbell and Jamie opens the door. He looks at Jan.

"What's *she* doing here?"

Tom looks into Jamie's eyes.

"Why did you take the time capsule?"

"Because it's ours – not yours."

"It's not ours. It belongs to Jan."

Pauly calls from the top of the stairs.

"Let them in, Jamie."

Jamie reluctantly• lets them into the house and follows them up the stairs to Pauly's room. There are musical instruments everywhere. There's a Spanish guitar and an electric guitar with an amplifier•. There are some bongo drums and an electric piano. Jan can't believe it.

"Wow, Pauly. Can you play all these instruments?"

"Yeah. I play and Jamie sings. Tom does the electrics. He's the technician•."

There are two shelves filled with LP records•. Jan starts looking at some of the covers•.

"There are some really old classics• here!"

Jamie and Pauly exchange looks. Pauly says: "They're all new albums, Jan. You don't know much about music, do you?"

- **amplifier:** piece of equipment to make sounds louder
- **classics:** well-known songs or films
- **covers:** the front of LPs or CDs
- **LP records:** old 12-inch vinyl records that existed before CDs
- **reluctantly:** not wanting to do something
- **technician:** the person who controls electrical equipment

"I know more than you think. So what kind of music do you play? Hip Hop? Rap? House Music?"

"What's House Music?" Pauly asks.

"Music you play in your house?" Jamie asks.

Jan takes the first album from the shelf and Tom puts it on the record deck•. It's *Abba*. The first track• on side 1• starts playing. It's *Mamma Mia*.

"I love this song," Jan says. "Now listen and watch. This technique is called 'scratching'." Jan puts her hand on the side of the record and moves it backwards and forwards, creating a new rhythm and sound.

GLOSSARY

- **deck:** where you play records
- **side 1:** one side of an old vinyl record
- **track:** a song or piece of music on a CD or LP

"You're breaking the record! Don't!" Jamie protests.

Pauly interrupts. "No. Listen, Jamie. It sounds amazing•."

Jan smiles at Pauly.

"It sounds really good if you rap too. Can you rap, Jamie?"

"I don't know. How do you rap?" Jamie asks.

"You don't sing – you speak to a rhythm and try to make your words rhyme•. Wait."

Jan stops the Abba record and starts a rhythm, making percussion• sounds with her voice. She stops and explains.

"This is called beatboxing. Can you try it, Pauly?"

Jan starts beatboxing and Pauly beatboxes too.

- **amazing:** fantastic
- **percussion:** musical instruments including drums
- **rhyme:** when a word has the same sound as another word

crew heart rap

I've come from the future,
I've travelled in time,
Now I'm stuck• in the past,
Trying to make my words rhyme.

I'm not on a mission•,
I haven't got a plan.
I'm just a normal schoolgirl
And my name is Jan.

Ladies and gentlemen,
Let me introduce to you:
Tom, Pauly and Jamie –
My three-man crew•.

Don't ever forget, boys
What I taught you tonight.
Keep scratching, beatboxing
And write
Your rap,
Say what you feel,
Speak from the heart,
And make it real.
The end,
My friend!

GLOSSARY

- **crew:** people working together
- **mission:** specific job to complete
- **stuck:** can't move

MUSIC

Do you play an instrument?

Do you sing?

Do you beatbox?

What music to do you like to listen to?

Talk to a friend.

Pauly, Jamie and Tom start cheering• and clapping• their hands. Jan takes a bow•, imagining she's performing in a big concert hall. She turns to Jamie.

"What did you say, Jamie? *I don't know much about music*?"

"OK. I'm sorry."

"Thank you. Now... I think you have something of mine."

Jamie's face turns red. He goes to Pauly's bed and brings out the biscuit tin from under it. He gives the tin to Jan.

"Can I have something from your time capsule to remember you?"

Jan smiles and opens the tin.

"Of course you can. Let's see... How about this?"

She takes out the rubber Earth Hour wristband. Jamie looks puzzled.

"What is it?"

"It's my Earth Hour wristband. You wear it like this."

She puts the wristband on Jamie's wrist.

"What's Earth Hour?"

"People around the world turn their lights off for one hour at the same time on the same day. It sends a message to world leaders• to stop climate change."

"What's climate change?"

"It's... something you need to stop. Don't you have a Green Day at school?"

Jamie smiles. "Green Day. That's a great name for a pop group. Thanks, Jan."

GLOSSARY

- **bow:** movement of lowering the top half of your body
- **cheering:** making a sound when you like or support something
- **clapping:** hitting your hands together to make a noise
- **leaders:** people in control of a group or country

Jan takes the Mika CD from the tin and gives it to Pauly.

"And this is for you."

"What is it?"

"It's a record of the future. It's a CD – a compact disc. Mika is a singer. He had problems at school too, Pauly. But he became a big pop star. I think you're going to be a pop star too."

"He looks like Leo Sayer."

"Leo *who*?"

Pauly shows Jan a record from his collection. It's called *You Make Me Feel Like Dancing* by Leo Sayer. There's a picture of Leo Sayer on the record cover. He's got big curly hair and looks like Mika.

"Take it. It's for you."

"Thanks, Pauly."

"Missed your bus again, have you?"

Tom's dad smiles when Jan arrives home with Tom again. Tom's mum appears from the kitchen.

"We saw Pauly's mother in town. She didn't know Pauly had a cold. You didn't lie• to us, did you, Tom?"

Dad turns his attention to Jan.

"You can stay here tonight, Jan. But tomorrow you should• go home. Your parents are probably very worried. You understand, don't you?"

Jan nods her head.

"You're very kind," she says. "Thank you."

Jan decides to go to bed early. Jan lies in bed, looking at the photos on her phone. She looks for a long time at the picture of her parents and then smiles when she sees the photo of Tom in the living room. Then she goes to sleep.

Sunday, 29 February 1976

A loud noise wakes Jan up suddenly. What time is it? She looks at the alarm clock beside the bed. It's five o'clock. Then she hears the noise again. It's thunder. Then she hears a different noise. It's the sound of something hitting the window. She gets up and goes to the window. She can see Tom standing outside in the rain. He's shouting at Jan, telling her to come outside.

GLOSSARY

- **lie:** say something that isn't true
- **should:** (here) it is best that you

Jan gets dressed, puts on her anorak and goes downstairs quietly, trying not to wake Tom's parents. She meets Tom outside.

"What are you doing, Tom?"

"The storm," he says. "It's the same storm as Thursday night. Let's go to the tree. Maybe you can go home!"

Jan follows Tom down the road then she remembers something.

"The time capsule!"

Tom shows her the biscuit tin under his jacket. "I've got it."

They walk quickly back down the road past Jamie's house and Pauly's house. It seems so long since she arrived here in the past. And now maybe there's the possibility she can return to the future. Soon they come to the river and then the old abandoned building. They run up the path through the trees and arrive at the piece of land with the apple tree.

WHAT'S GOING TO HAPPEN NEXT?

Is Jan going to get back to 2010?

Is Tom going to go with her?

"Now what do we do?" asks Jan.

"I put the time capsule back where I found it and..."

"And I go home."

"Yes."

Tom uses his hands to dig a hole by the tree. He buries the time capsule and then stands up.

Jan suddenly realises something.

"Tom! I wanted to give you something from the time capsule."

"No, it's OK. I don't want anything. It's more important for you to go home."

Jan feels disappointed that Tom doesn't want something to remember her. But he's right. The important thing is to get home.

"I'm never going to forget you, Tom. Thanks. You're a real friend."

"Bye, Jan. Look for me in the future. Promise•?"

"I promise."

Then he turns and runs back to the trees. Jan watches his shadow disappear into the trees. A sudden flash of lightning illuminates the scene followed by a loud crash of thunder. Jan looks round and sees her house. She's back in the garden of her house in Hampton Street.

Sunday, 28 February 2010

Jan runs across to the house and opens the door to the kitchen. Her mum and dad are in the kitchen. Dad is on the phone.

"No. We don't know anything. The police are looking now. Yes… Wait!"

GLOSSARY

- **promise:** say you will definitely do it

Dad sees Jan. He puts down the phone and runs across to her. He puts his arms around her and holds her tightly•. Jan feels safe again. Now her mother is holding her too and kissing her. It feels good to be home.

WHAT'S 'HOME' FOR YOU?

- ☐ A building in which I live
- ☐ Being with the people I love
- ☐ Having my own personal space

"Jan. Are you all right? What happened?"

"I'm all right."

"You're safe. We were so worried."

"Where were you? We tried to find you with the Kiwi key ring but there was no signal."

Jan takes off her anorak and sits down at the kitchen table. She knows she can't tell her parents the truth. Who's going to believe her if she says she travelled back in time to 1976? So she says:

"I can't remember, but I'm OK. Really. I'm very tired. Can I go to bed?"

"Of course you can."

Jan goes up to her room but she doesn't go to bed. She stands at the window, watching the apple tree, thinking of her three new friends – Tom, Pauly and Jamie.

GLOSSARY

- **tightly:** strongly; close to him

SEARCHING FOR TOM

11 The next day is Monday but Jan doesn't go to school. Mum and dad say she can stay at home until she feels ready to go back to school. A policewoman comes to the house and asks her lots of questions but she answers all her questions with the same answer: "I'm sorry. I can't remember."

After the policewoman goes and her parents are busy talking to uncles, aunts, grandfathers, cousins and other relatives• on the phone, Jan goes out into the garden. She looks at the apple tree. Was it all a dream? Did she really travel back in time? She looks carefully at the tree and then she sees it – Tom's name carved in the tree trunk.

She digs up the time capsule and takes it up to her room.

If she really travelled to the past then the Mika CD and Earth Hour wristband aren't going to be inside the tin. She puts the biscuit tin on the table and opens it very carefully.

But there's a surprise waiting for her inside the time capsule. None of her things are there.
"What?!"

• **relatives:** people who are part of your family

But there are other different things inside the time capsule. She takes them out one by one• and puts them on the table. There's a copy of Pauly's record by Leo Sayer – *You Make Me Feel Like Dancing*. There's a penknife•. There's a 1975 map of Port Prime and a copy of the *Prime News* newspaper. She looks at the date on the newspaper – February 27th, 1976. And there's a letter from Tom to Jan. She opens the letter and starts reading.

GLOSSARY

- **one by one:** one thing and then another thing
- **penknife:** a small knife you can carry

Dear Jan,

I hope you arrive home safely and your parents aren't too angry. And I hope you like the things in the time capsule. The knife is my special penknife. I used it to cut my name in your apple tree. The map is for you to remember what Port Prime was like when you were here – before the airport and the motorway. Look carefully. I put a cross• on the cliffs where we cycled on Saturday. I put in the Leo Sayer record that Pauly gave you. And the newspaper is Friday's paper. Look at the TV page for Doctor Who in The Seeds of Doom. I can't believe Doctor Who is still on TV in 2010!!!

I'm sorry I took the things from your time capsule. I hope you understand. Don't forget. Look for me in the future. I know you can find me if you try.

Your best friend,

Tom

• **cross:** written mark or sign made of two lines crossing

Jan puts the things back in the box. Suddenly she remembers the photo of Tom on her phone. She looks at the photo of Tom sitting on the sofa in his living room and she says: "How can I find you, Tom?"

She thinks of searching on Google but there are millions of people called Tom and she doesn't know his surname. She thinks of going to his parents' house but the town council pulled down those houses years ago when they built the motorway. And then she remembers something – the Kiwi key ring. Tom has the key ring from the time capsule. If she enters the key number at the Kiwi Internet site, maybe she can find him.

Jan logs on to the Internet and goes to the Kiwi Technology website. She follows the links• to the key ring section of the site. The page asks Jan to enter the key ring number. Her dad used the same number as her phone to make it easy to remember. She enters the number and clicks• on 'Go!'. A few seconds later a message appears:

> Kiwi key ring located•!
> The Kiwi key ring you are looking for is located at Kiwi Technology, Port Prime.

Jan stares at the computer screen. "Oh, no!" she thinks. "It's not working•." But then she thinks: "Maybe Tom works at Kiwi."

GLOSSARY

- **clicks:** presses a button on the mouse to connect to an Internet link
- **links:** words, pictures or icons on an Internet page that take you to another page
- **located:** found
- **working:** functioning correctly

SEARCHING THE NET

In which order does Jan do these actions? Number them.

- ☐ type in the website address
- ☐ enter the key ring number
- ☐ log on to the Internet
- ☐ follow the link
- ☐ click 'Go!'

She goes downstairs and finds her mum and dad having coffee in the kitchen.

"Mum? Dad? Is there anyone at Kiwi called Tom?"

Her mum looks at dad, surprised by the question.

"Why... yes. There are a few people called Tom working there."

"There's Tom Bradley in our department... and Thomas Duncan in accounts... and Tom Green, of course."

"Who's Tom Green?" Jan asks.

"Michael Green's father, you know, the boy in your class at school."

Jan can see Michael smiling at her from the back of the classroom and suddenly there's something familiar about his face.

"Yes. It's him!"

"Michael Green?"

"No. *Tom* Green. I'm going to see him," Jan says excitedly.

"You can't see Tom Green. He's the head• of the company. He started the company. He's an important man."

• **head:** the director or top person

But Jan doesn't listen. She runs out of the house, takes her bicycle from the garage, and cycles down the road, through the centre of town, past the school and up the private road to Kiwi Technology, the big glass building at the top of the hill.

The man in reception• looks up at Jan.
"Can I help you?"
"I want to see Tom Green, please."
"Do you have an appointment•?"
"No. Tell him Jan is here to see him. He knows who I am."

The man picks up a phone and calls a number.
"Excuse me, sir. There's a girl in reception who wants to see you. Her name is Jan... Yes... I see... Very good, sir." He hangs up• the phone and looks at Jan. "Take the lift to the sixth floor."

GLOSSARY

- **appointment:** an agreed time to see someone
- **hangs up:** ends the phone conversation
- **reception:** area at the entrance of a building where you are greeted

A SURPRISE DISCOVERY

12 The lift doors open and a woman is waiting outside.

"You must be Jan. I'm Laura, Mr Green's personal assistant. Please follow me. He's expecting you•."

Jan follows Laura down a very long corridor to a big office. One of the walls is a window with a spectacular• view of the town, the cliffs, the airport, and the town of Apsworth. Jan thinks she can even see the sea in the distance. A man is sitting behind a desk. He's about fifty years old but Jan recognises him immediately. It's Tom.

"Hello Jan," Tom says. "I knew you'd find me."

He looks at something on his desk. It's a glass case•. Inside the case is Jan's Kiwi key ring. The locator light on the key ring is flashing•.

"Please. Sit down."

- **case:** box
- **expecting you:** waiting for you to arrive
- **flashing:** going on and off
- **spectacular:** very impressive

Jan sits down.
"I don't understand," she says.
"You're as white as a sheet•. Have some water."
Tom pours Jan a glass of water. She drinks it all.

SAYINGS WITH COLOURS

Complete the idioms with these words:
a beetroot   grass   coal

as **green** as ....
as **black** as ....
as **red** as ....

"Let me explain. When you arrived in 1976 you changed my life. You gave me a vision of the world in the future. And I wanted to be part of that future. You know how much I loved electronics and building things. So I studied the objects in your time capsule. I took them apart• and I put them together• again. I tried to understand how they worked and I started to make gadgets of my own. A lot of them didn't work. But then I created a portable music device."
"The Kiwi player."

GLOSSARY

- **put them together:** used all the pieces to make an object
- **took them apart:** removed all the pieces
- **white as a sheet:** when a person's face is extremely white (as a sheet on a bed)

"That's right. I started the business. The player was a success. And the rest is history."

"But you stole those things from me."

"I didn't steal them. *You* put them in the time capsule, remember? I used them to help me invent things."

"This is very confusing."

Jan gets up and walks to the window.

"My mum and dad work for you. Why?"

"You told me, remember? You said they worked for Kiwi. So when I started the business, I knew I had to find your parents. It wasn't difficult. Remember this?"

Tom takes a picture from a drawer. It's a postcard – the postcard from Jan's aunt, Suzie.

"When the Berlin Wall came down in 1989 I found your aunt. As you said, she was a very famous reporter. Your aunt introduced me to your mother. I offered her a job in the company and she accepted."

"And dad?"

"Your mother met your father while she was working here."

"It's incredible."

"Incredible but true."

"What about Pauly and Jamie?"

"They became very successful DJs and record producers•. I think they made more money than I did. They live in New York now."

"I think I need to go. This is all very strange."

"I understand."

Jan gets up and walks to the door. Before she leaves, she looks back at Tom.

"Did you ever fly on Concorde?

"Yes, I did," Tom smiles.

"One other thing, Jan. Thank you for being nice to Michael. I appreciate it. And he likes you a lot."

"I like Michael. He reminds me of you – when you were a boy."

"I wanted to call him Mika but his mother said *no*. So we called him Michael instead."

When Jan gets home, her mum and dad are waiting for her.

GLOSSARY

- **record producers:** people who help musicians to find finances and who organise their recordings in a studio

They say they need to talk to her so they all sit down at the kitchen table. There's an old envelope• on the table.

"What's in the envelope?" Jan asks.

Jan's mum pushes the envelope towards Jan.

"We don't know," she says. "When I started working at Kiwi, before you were born, Tom Green gave me this envelope. He told me to give it to my daughter when she became eighteen. I don't know how he knew about you."

Dad reaches across the table and takes Jan's hand.

"We know you're not eighteen yet but we feel this is the right time for you to open the envelope."

Jan nervously takes the envelope and opens it slowly. She looks inside and takes out some official papers.

"What are these?" she asks. "They look like legal• documents."

Jan's dad starts looking at the documents. He looks surprised and then shocked•.

"What's wrong? What is it?"

"According to these papers, Jan owns 50% of Kiwi Technology. Tom Green owns the rest."

- **envelope:** paper container for a letter
- **legal:** related to the law
- **shocked:** very surprised

Jan's mum looks serious.
"I think it's a good idea if we don't say anything about this. Let's put the documents back in the envelope, put the envelope back in the cupboard and forget about it until Jan is eighteen."

Jan agrees to keep the secret. She wants life to be normal again but she wonders if life is ever going to be normal again.
"Tomorrow," she thinks, "I'm going to go with Michael to the cliffs and show him where the sea was in the past. It's going to be a good day."

After Reading

Personal Response

1 Read each statement and circle the number that is most true for you.

1 = absolutely not 5 = very much

a It's a good story.
1 2 3 4 5

b It's easy to understand.
1 2 3 4 5

c I know lots of new words.
1 2 3 4 5

d I want to give it to a friend.
1 2 3 4 5

2 Were the predictions you made about the story on page 10 correct?

3 Which characters did you like best?

4 Do you want to travel in time?

5 Do you prefer the future or the past?

6 What historic event would you like to see?

After Reading

Comprehension

1 Are these sentences true (T) or false (F)? Tick (✔)

	T	F
a Jan's mum likes reading.	☐	☐
b Jan's time capsule is for a Science project in school.	☐	☐
c Jan uses a cardboard box for her time capsule.	☐	☐
d Jan's aunt Suzie is a History teacher.	☐	☐
e There is nothing to do in Port Prime.	☐	☐
f Jan got lost when the family was on holiday in Scotland.	☐	☐
g Jan buries the biscuit tin beside an apple tree.	☐	☐
h Jan is the only student in her class to complete the time capsule project.	☐	☐
i Jan travels into the future during a thunderstorm.	☐	☐
j Tom, Pauly and Jamie think that Jan is mad.	☐	☐
k There is a computer in Tom's bedroom.	☐	☐
l Both Jan and Tom go to PPC School.	☐	☐
m Jan teaches the boys how to rap.	☐	☐
n Tom makes a new time capsule for Jan.	☐	☐
o In the future Tom becomes a famous rapper.	☐	☐
p At the end of the story Jan is eighteen years old.	☐	☐

2 Correct the false sentences.

3 **Write Jan's diary for the days of the story.**

THURSDAY Today I ... ______________________

____

FRIDAY ______________________

____

SATURDAY ______________________

____

SUNDAY ______________________

____

MONDAY ______________________

____

4 **Look at this picture from 1976.**
Describe it.
How is your living room different now?

Which do you prefer?

Share your ideas with a partner.

After Reading

Characters

1 Complete the facts with the name of the character.

a .... belongs to a book group.
b .... is good at inventing stories.
c .... is a vegetarian.
d .... has problems at home.
e .... likes the Twilight books and films.
f .... is always late for work or working on a secret project.
g .... wants to be a news reporter in the future.
h .... wants to be a pop star but has problems at school.
i .... wants to work in electronics in the future.
l .... loves reading.

2 Jan influences what Tom, Jamie and Pauly do in the future. Write how she influences each one.

....

....

....

3 Match each quote with one of the names below.

Jan	Michael Green	Tom	Mrs Zinger	Jamie	Tom's mum

a Our lives today are going to be tomorrow's history.

....

b You can't tell people you're from the future.

....

c Girls aren't allowed in here!

....

d I know how it feels to be alone.

....

e I think I'm in the future.

....

f Are you all right, my love? You look ill.

....

4 With a partner say when the people in Exercise 3 say these things and who they say them to.

After Reading

Plot and Theme

1 What happens in the story? Put the sentences in the correct order.

1	2	3	4	5	6	7	8	9	10	11
a										

a Jan's mother gives her a biscuit tin for her time capsule.

b Jan goes with Tom to the cliffs.

c Jan performs a rap for Pauly and Jamie.

d Jan returns to the present time.

e Jan talks to Michael Green after History class.

f Jan talks to a policewoman.

g Jan travels in time for the first time.

h Jan writes a letter to someone in the future.

i Jan goes to Kiwi Technology.

j Tom buries the time capsule.

k Jan meets Tom, Pauly and Jamie.

13 **2 Listen and check your answers.**

3 Write a letter from Jan to Aunt Suzie describing what happened.

4 One of the themes of the story is the difference between the past and the present. In 2010 the *UK Office for National Statistics* compared life in the 1970s with life today. What did they discover? Complete the sentences with either *Then* or *Now* and choose the past or the present of the verbs.

a .... people *live / lived* longer.

b .... people *are / were* thinner.

c .... more people *go / went* on holiday abroad.

d .... there *are / were* more divorces.

e .... more people *go / went* to church.

f .... there *isn't / wasn't* so much technology.

g .... people *earn / earned* more money.

h .... more people *are / were* unemployed.

i .... fewer people *are / were* getting married.

j .... more children *walk / walked* to school.

5 Was life in the 1970s better than life today? Use the prompts from the story to write sentences comparing the 1970s to the present. Share with a partner.

a Smoking

b Television

c LPs/CDs/downloads

d Rap, house music, punk

e Mobile phones

f Internet

g Food

h Friends & freedom

After Reading

Language

Cardinal and ordinal numbers

1 Use the words from the story to complete the sentences.

anorak   beatboxing   en-suite   gadgets   kiwi   shadow

a All the hotel rooms are ....

b He has the latest phone, games and music players. He loves ....

c It's going to rain. You should wear your ....

d Our cat is frightened by its own ....

e Have you heard her .... ? She's fantastic.

f Have you ever eaten .... fruit?

2 Use the words to complete the extracts from the story.

aerials   battery   button   cable   enters   logs on   memory stick   signal

Jan **a** .... to her computer and copies her photo collection onto the **b** ....

If you ever get lost, you press the red **c** .... on the key ring and it sends a **d** .... to another person. The other person then logs on to the Kiwi Internet site and **e** .... the key ring code to find out where you are.

Tom studies Jan's phone.
"There's no **f** ...."
"It has a **g** .... to give it power. It uses **h** .... for communication."

Look + preposition

3 Choose the correct form of the adjective.

1 Mrs Zinger's classes are always *interesting / interested.*

2 Mum looks up from her book. Suddenly she's*interesting / interested.*

3 "The future is an *exciting / excited* place," Jan thinks as she gets out of bed.

4 When she comes to the building, she hears *exciting / excited* voices from inside.

5 Tom's dad looks *puzzling / puzzled.* "Why can't she stay with Pauly?"

6 "No. Listen, Jamie. It sounds *amazing / amazed.*"

4 Use the verbs in the present continuous to complete the description of the pictures on the biscuit tin.

build carry play sit walk

1 Children .... in the snow.

2 A family .... around a living-room fire.

3 A boy and girl .... a snowman.

4 A man .... past the shop windows.

5 He .... a Christmas tree home.

5 Find a word in the second box that rhymes with a word in the first box. Draw lines.

end	crew
feel	friend
time	real
tonight	rhyme
you	write

After Reading

Exit Test

1 Listen and choose the correct picture.

a 1 

2 

b 1 

2 

c 1 

2 

d 1 

2 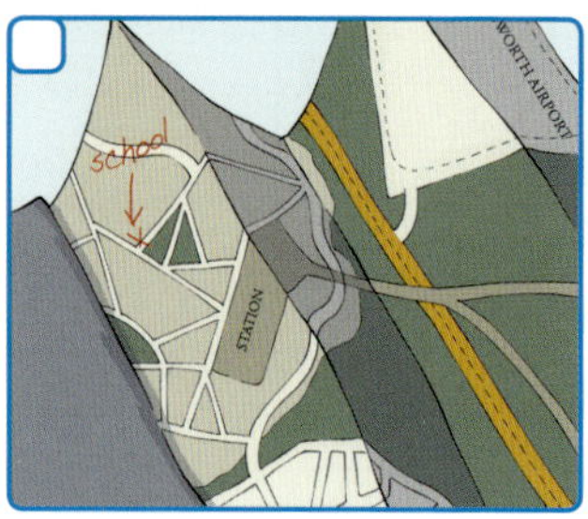

2 **Look at the picture. What does Jan put in her time capsule?**

3 **With a partner choose one of the things and get him/her to guess it.**

No.

Can you listen to it?

4 **Tom used some information that Jan gave him to become successful. Do you think he was right or wrong to do this? Explain why.**

Which decade are you from?

Answer these questions and discover which decade you really come from.

1 Choose a fashion item.

- ☐ **A** leather jacket
- ☐ **B** mini skirt
- ☐ **C** jeans
- ☐ **D** leg warmers
- ☐ **E** flannel shirt

2 Which singer/group do you like best?

- ☐ **A** Elvis
- ☐ **B** The Beatles
- ☐ **C** Donna Summer
- ☐ **D** Madonna
- ☐ **E** Aerosmith

3 Choose your favourite cartoon.

- ☐ **A** Tom & Jerry
- ☐ **B** The Flintstones
- ☐ **C** Scooby Doo
- ☐ **D** The Smurfs
- ☐ **E** The Simpsons

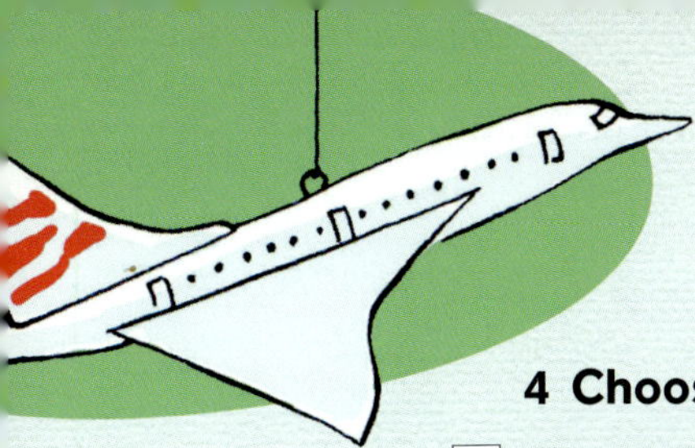

4 Choose an event you would like to see.

- [ ] **A** The first passenger airplane in the air.
- [ ] **B** The first man on the Moon.
- [ ] **C** The first cell phone call.
- [ ] **D** The first personal computers in the stores.
- [ ] **E** The first web browser to search the Internet.

5 Which is the coolest invention?

- [ ] **A** Colour TV
- [ ] **B** Computer mouse
- [ ] **C** Video games
- [ ] **D** Compact disks (CDs)
- [ ] **E** Memory stick

Mostly As

You are from the 1950s.

Mostly Bs

You are from the 1960s.

Mostly Cs

You are from the 1970s.

Mostly Ds

YOU ARE FROM THE 1980S.

Mostly Es

You are from the 1990s.

After Reading

Project

1 Choose one of the following projects.

1970s

My world in the 1970s

Where do you live? What was it like in the 1970s? Try to find maps and photographs to discover the changes during the past 40 years.

- Use the Internet to search for images and news stories.
- Ask your family and friends.
- Find out about places, fashion, music, politics...

Make a time capsule

Make your own real time capsule and hide or bury it somewhere for people to find in the future.

- Find a container (make sure you have permission to use it)
- Decide what to put inside.
- Write a letter to the person who will find it. Remember to include information about the objects inside the time capsule.
- Hide the time capsule or bury it somewhere.